# HEALING SCRIPTURES

ELIZABETH ANNE REEVES

WESTBOW
PRESS®
A DIVISION OF THOMAS NELSON
& ZONDERVAN

Copyright © 2023 Elizabeth Anne Reeves.

All rights reserved. No part of this book may be used or reproduced by any means, graphic, electronic, or mechanical, including photocopying, recording, taping or by any information storage retrieval system without the written permission of the author except in the case of brief quotations embodied in critical articles and reviews.

This book is a work of non-fiction. Unless otherwise noted, the author and the publisher make no explicit guarantees as to the accuracy of the information contained in this book and in some cases, names of people and places have been altered to protect their privacy.

WestBow Press books may be ordered through booksellers or by contacting:

WestBow Press
A Division of Thomas Nelson & Zondervan
1663 Liberty Drive
Bloomington, IN 47403
www.westbowpress.com
844-714-3454

Because of the dynamic nature of the Internet, any web addresses or links contained in this book may have changed since publication and may no longer be valid. The views expressed in this work are solely those of the author and do not necessarily reflect the views of the publisher, and the publisher hereby disclaims any responsibility for them.

Any people depicted in stock imagery provided by Getty Images are models, and such images are being used for illustrative purposes only. Certain stock imagery © Getty Images.

Interior Image Credit: Elizabeth Anne Reeves

Scripture texts in this work are taken from the New American Bible, revised edition © 2010, 1991, 1986, 1970 Confraternity of Christian Doctrine, Washington, D.C. and are used by permission of the copyright owner. All Rights Reserved. No part of the New American Bible may be reproduced in any form without permission in writing from the copyright owner.

ISBN: 978-1-6642-6294-2 (sc)
ISBN: 978-1-6642-6295-9 (hc)
ISBN: 978-1-6642-6293-5 (e)

Print information available on the last page.

WestBow Press rev. date: 05/03/2023

...God anointed Jesus of Nazareth with the Holy Spirit and power. He went about doing good and healing all those oppressed by the devil, for God was with him. (Acts 10:38)

*Nihil Obstat:*
Susan M. Timoney, S.T.D. Censor Deputatus

*Imprimatur:*
Most Rev. Martin D. Holley Auxiliary Bishop of Washington

Archdiocese of Washington May 15, 2014
The *nihil obstat* and *imprimatur* are official declarations that a book or pamphlet is free of doctrinal or moral error. There is no implication that those who have granted the *nihil obstat* and the *imprimatur* agree with the content, opinions or statements expressed therein.

**HEALING ROSARY**
**Elizabeth Anne Reeves © 2022**

This book is dedicated to my father,
**Thomas Garner Reeves, Jr.**
who knelt by my bedside when I was
3 years old and taught me to pray.

# Author's Note

This *Healing Rosary* booklet is dedicated to three Roman Catholic Priests who were involved in healing ministries. Father John Lubey taught me about the powerful role of the Virgin Mary in the New Testament. Father George Joyce taught me about the presence of Christ in the breaking of bread. Father Edward McDonough taught me the power of the Holy Spirit in healing. I am alive today in part because of their prayers.

Section 1, page 100 in *The Manual of Indulgences,* issued by the United States Conference of Catholic Bishops (USCCB) in 1999, reads: "A plenary indulgence is granted to the faithful who read the Sacred Scriptures as spiritual reading, from a text approved by competent authority and with the reverence due to the divine word, for at least a half an hour; if the time is less, the indulgence will be partial." The translation used for all Bible quotations is the New American Bible (NAB) approved by the USCCB. It is this author's hope that readers will reverently read these accounts of Jesus Christ's medical miracles on earth and be inspired to pray for healing.

The front and back of the *Healing Rosary* booklet contain images of the Green Scapular. The Green Scapular of the Immaculate Heart of Mary is a Roman Catholic devotional. The Green Scapular was approved by Pope Pius IX in 1863 and again in 1870.

The Blessed Virgin Mary, in an apparition on September 8, 1840, the Feast of her Nativity, appeared to Sister Justine Bisqueyburu, a religious of the Daughters of Charity of Saint Vincent de Paul. She entrusted the Green Scapular of her Immaculate Heart to Sister Justine for circulation to contribute to the conversion of souls, particularly those who have no faith, and to procure for them a happy death.

Father McDonough told me he distributed them to persons or their loved ones who needed healing. The only requirement is that the Green Scapular be blessed by a priest and worn or carried by the person wishing to benefit by it.

The practice of asking for the intercession of the saints is millennia old and is based on Hebrews 12:1: "Therefore, since we are surrounded by so great a cloud of witnesses, let us rid ourselves of very burden and sin that clings to us, and preserve in running the race that lies before us."

Acts 19:11–12 says, "God wrought special miracles by the hands of Paul; so that from his body were brought unto the sick handkerchiefs or aprons, and the diseases departed from them, and the evil spirits went out of them."

Paul touched these clothes, also called "aprons and handkerchiefs," which were distributed to those who were sick. According to Matthew 9:20 and Matthew 14:35–37, many people were healed by Jesus when they touched His clothes

## Church of the Nativity in Bethlehem

# Contents

The following is a listing of the twenty-two medical miracles of Jesus with corresponding scriptures.

> Now Jesus did many other signs in the presence of [his] disciples that are not written in this book. But these are written that you may [come to] believe that Jesus is the Messiah, the Son of God, and that through this belief you may have life in his name. (John 20:30, 31)

| | | |
|---|---|---|
| 1 | Nobleman's Son at Capernaum—First Decade | 2 |
| 2 | Man with Leprosy—Second Decade | 5 |
| 3 | Roman Centurion's Servant—Third Decade | 8 |
| 4 | Peter's Mother-In-Law—Fourth Decade | 12 |
| 5 | The Healing of a Paralytic—Fifth Decade | 15 |
| 6 | Jairus' Daughter—Sixth Decade | 19 |
| 7 | Woman with Hemorrhage—Seventh Decade | 22 |
| 8 | Woman's Daughter—Eighth Decade | 26 |
| 9 | Blind Man at Bethsaida—Ninth Decade | 29 |
| 10 | Sick Man at the Pool of Bethsaida—Tenth Decade | 33 |
| 11 | Man Born Blind—Eleventh Decade | 36 |
| 12 | Crippled Woman—Twelfth Decade | 39 |
| 13 | Man with Edema—Thirteenth Decade | 43 |
| 14 | Ten Men with Leprosy—Fourteenth Decade | 46 |
| 15 | Bartimaeus—Fifteenth Decade | 49 |
| 16 | The Man with a Withered Hand—Sixteenth Decade | 52 |
| 17 | The Healing of Two Blind Men—Seventeenth Decade | 55 |
| 18 | The Healing of the Blind Beggar—Eighteenth Decade | 59 |
| 19 | Healing of the Ear of Malchus—Nineteenth Decade | 62 |
| 20 | Raising the Dead | 66 |

### *Apostles' Creed*

*I believe in God, the Father Almighty, Creator of heaven and earth; and in Jesus Christ, His only Son, our Lord: Who was conceived by the Holy Spirit, born of the Virgin Mary; suffered under Pontius Pilate, was crucified, died and was buried. He Descended into hell; the third day He rose again from the dead; He ascended into heaven, is seated at the right hand of God the Father Almighty; from thence He shall come to judge the living and the dead. I believe in the Holy Spirit, the Holy Catholic Church, the communion of Saints, the forgiveness of sins, the resurrection of the body, and life everlasting. Amen*

### *Our Father*

*Our Father who art in Heaven, hallowed be thy name; Thy kingdom come Thy will be done on earth as it is in heaven. Give us this day our daily bread; and forgive us our trespasses as we forgive those who trespass against us; and lead us not into temptation but deliver us from evil. Amen*

### *Three Hail Marys*

*Hail Mary, full of grace. The Lord is with thee. Blessed art thou amongst women, and blessed is the fruit of thy womb, Jesus.*

*Holy Mary, Mother of God, pray for us sinners, now and at the hour of our death. Amen.*

### *Glory Be*

*Glory be to the Father, and to the Son, and to the Holy Spirit, as it was in the beginning, is now, and ever shall be, world without end. Amen.*

### *Fatima Prayer*

*O my Jesus, forgive us our sins, save us from the fires of hell, and lead all souls to Heaven, especially those in most need of Your Mercy. Amen*

**Temple at Capernaum
Across from St Peter's Home**

# First Miracle Healing of Jesus

# Nobleman's Son at Capernaum—First Decade

## John 4:46–54

46 Then he returned to Cana in Galilee, where he had made the water wine. Now there was a royal official whose son was ill in Capernaum.

47 When he heard that Jesus had arrived in Galilee from Judea, he went to him and asked him to come down and heal his son, who was near death.

48 Jesus said to him, "Unless you people see signs and wonders, you will not believe."

49 The royal official said to him, "Sir, come down before my child dies."

50 Jesus said to him, "You may go; your son will live." The man believed what Jesus said to him and left.

51 While he was on his way back, his slaves met him and told him that his boy would live.

52 He asked them when he began to recover. They told him, "The fever left him yesterday, about one in the afternoon."

53 The father realized that just at that time Jesus had said to him, "Your son will live," and he and his whole household came to believe.

54 [Now] this was the second sign Jesus did when he came to Galilee from Judea.

*Our Father who art in Heaven, hallowed be thy name; Thy kingdom come Thy will be done on earth as it is in heaven. Give us this day our daily bread; and forgive us our trespasses as we forgive those who trespass against us; and lead us not into temptation but deliver us from evil. Amen*

*Repeat ten times:*

*Hail Mary, full of grace. The Lord is with thee. Blessed art thou amongst women, and blessed is the fruit of thy womb, Jesus.*
    *Holy Mary, Mother of God, pray for us sinners, now and at the hour of our death. Amen.*

*Glory be to the Father, and to the Son, and to the Holy Spirit, as it was in the beginning, is now, and ever shall be, world without end. Amen.*

*O my Jesus, forgive us our sins, save us from the fires of hell, and lead all souls to Heaven, especially those in most need of Your Mercy. Amen*

## SECOND MIRACLE HEALING OF JESUS

ELIZABETH ANNE REEVES

# Man with Leprosy—Second Decade

## Matthew 8:1–4; see also Mark 1:40–44 and Luke 5:12–14

1. When Jesus came down from the mountain, great crowds followed him.
2. And then a leper approached, did him homage, and said, "Lord, if you wish, you can make me clean."
3. He stretched out his hand, touched him, and said, "I will do it. Be made clean." His leprosy was cleansed immediately.
4. Then Jesus said to him, "See that you tell no one, but go show yourself to the priest, and offer the gift that Moses prescribed; that will be proof for them."

*Our Father who art in Heaven, hallowed be thy name; Thy kingdom come Thy will be done on earth as it is in heaven. Give us this day our daily bread; and forgive us our trespasses as we forgive those who trespass against us; and lead us not into temptation but deliver us from evil. Amen*

*Repeat ten times:*

*Hail Mary, full of grace. The Lord is with thee. Blessed art thou amongst women, and blessed is the fruit of thy womb, Jesus.*

*Holy Mary, Mother of God, pray for us sinners, now and at the hour of our death. Amen.*

*Glory be to the Father, and to the Son, and to the Holy Spirit, as it was in the beginning, is now, and ever shall be, world without end. Amen …*

*O my Jesus, forgive us our sins, save us from the fires of hell, and lead all souls to Heaven, especially those in most need of Your Mercy. Amen*

# Third Miracle Healing of Jesus

# Roman Centurion's Servant—Third Decade

## Matthew 8:5–13; see also Luke 7: 1–10

5     When he entered Capernaum, a centurion approached him and appealed to him,

6     Saying, "Lord, my servant is lying at home paralyzed, suffering dreadfully."

7     He said to him, "I will come and cure him."

8     The centurion said in reply, "Lord, I am not worthy to have you enter under my roof; only say the word and my servant will be healed.

9     For I too am a person subject to authority, with soldiers subject to me. And I say to one, 'Go,' and he goes; and to another, 'Come here,' and he comes; and to my slave, 'Do this,' and he does it."

10    When Jesus heard this, he was amazed and said to those following him, "Amen, I say to you, in no one in Israel have I found such faith.

11    I say to you, many will come from the east and the west, and will recline with Abraham, Isaac, and Jacob at the banquet in the kingdom of heaven,

12    But the children of the kingdom will be driven out into the outer darkness, where there will be wailing and grinding of teeth."

13    And Jesus said to the centurion, "You may go; as you have believed, let it be done for you." And at that very hour [his] servant was healed.

*Our Father who art in Heaven, hallowed be thy name; Thy kingdom come Thy will be done on earth as it is in heaven. Give us this day our daily bread; and forgive us our trespasses as we forgive those who trespass against us; and lead us not into temptation but deliver us from evil. Amen*

*Repeat ten times:*

*Hail Mary, full of grace. The Lord is with thee. Blessed art thou amongst women, and blessed is the fruit of thy womb, Jesus.*
    *Holy Mary, Mother of God, pray for us sinners, now and at the hour of our death. Amen.*

*Glory be to the Father, and to the Son, and to the Holy Spirit, as it was in the beginning, is now, and ever shall be, world without end. Amen.*

*O my Jesus, forgive us our sins, save us from the fires of hell, and lead all souls to Heaven, especially those in most need of Your Mercy. Amen*

## Birth Site of Jesus in Bethlehem

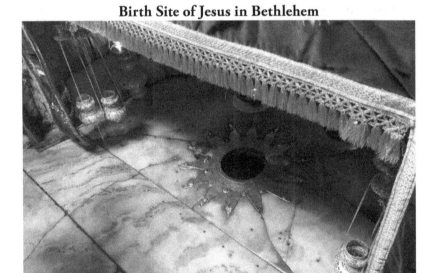

# Fourth Miracle Healing of Jesus

# Peter's Mother-In-Law—Fourth Decade

## Luke 4:38–39

38  After he left the synagogue, he entered the house of Simon. Simon's mother-in-law was afflicted with a severe fever, and they interceded with him about her.

## Matthew 8:14–15; see also Mark 1:30–31

14  Jesus entered the house of Peter and saw his mother-in-law lying in bed with a fever.
15  He touched her hand, the fever left her, and she rose and waited on him.

## Matthew 8:16–17 Other Healings

16  When it was evening, they brought him many who were possessed by demons, and he drove out the spirits by a word and cured all the sick,
17  to fulfill what had been said by Isaiah the prophet: "He took away our infirmities and bore our diseases."

*Our Father who art in Heaven, hallowed be thy name; Thy kingdom come Thy will be done on earth as it is in heaven. Give us this day our daily bread.*

*And forgive us our trespasses as we forgive those who trespass against us; And lead us not into temptation. But deliver us from evil. Amen*

*Repeat ten times:*

*Hail Mary, full of grace. The Lord is with thee. Blessed art thou amongst women, and blessed is the fruit of thy womb, Jesus.*

*Holy Mary, Mother of God, pray for us sinners, now and at the hour of our death. Amen.*

*Glory be to the Father, and to the Son, and to the Holy Spirit, as it was in the beginning, is now, and ever shall be, world without end. Amen…*

*O my Jesus, forgive us our sins, save us from the fires of hell, and lead all souls to Heaven, especially those in most need of Your Mercy. Amen*

# Fifth Miracle Healing of Jesus

ELIZABETH ANNE REEVES

# The Healing of a Paralytic—Fifth Decade

## Mark 2:3–12; see also Matthew 9:2–7 and Luke 5:18–25

3   They came bringing to him a paralytic carried by four men.

4   Unable to get near Jesus because of the crowd, they opened up the roof above him. After they had broken through, they let down the mat on which the paralytic was lying.

5   When Jesus saw their faith, he said to the paralytic, "Child, your sins are forgiven."

6   Now some of the scribes were sitting there asking themselves,

7   "Why does this man speak that way? He is blaspheming. Who but God alone can forgive sins?"

8   Jesus immediately knew in his mind what they were thinking to themselves, so he said, "Why are you thinking such things in your hearts?

9   Which is easier, to say to the paralytic, 'Your sins are forgiven,' or to say, 'Rise, pick up your mat and walk'?

10  But that you may know that the Son of Man has authority to forgive sins on earth"

11  he said to the paralytic, "I say to you, rise, pick up your mat, and go home."

*Our Father who art in Heaven, hallowed be thy name; Thy kingdom come Thy will be done on earth as it is in heaven. Give us this day our daily bread; and forgive us our trespasses as we forgive those who trespass against us; And lead us not into temptation, But deliver us from evil. Amen*

*Repeat ten times:*

*Hail Mary, full of grace. The Lord is with thee. Blessed art thou amongst women, and blessed is the fruit of thy womb, Jesus.*

    *Holy Mary, Mother of God, pray for us sinners, now and at the hour of our death. Amen.*

*Glory be to the Father, and to the Son, and to the Holy Spirit, as it was in the beginning, is now, and ever shall be, world without end. Amen.*

*O my Jesus, forgive us our sins, save us from the fires of hell, and lead all souls to Heaven, especially those in most need of Your Mercy. Amen*

## The Eastern Gate of Jerusalem
## Called the Golden Gate or Gate of Mercy

# Sixth Miracle Healing of Jesus

# Jairus' Daughter—Sixth Decade

## Mark 5:35–43

35  While he was still speaking, people from the synagogue official's house arrived and said, "Your daughter has died; why trouble the teacher any longer?"
36  Disregarding the message that was reported, Jesus said to the synagogue official, "Do not be afraid; just have faith."
37  He did not allow anyone to accompany him inside except Peter, James, and John, the brother of James.
38  When they arrived at the house of the synagogue official, he caught sight of a commotion, people weeping and wailing loudly.
39  So he went in and said to them, "Why this commotion and weeping? The child is not dead but asleep."
40  And they ridiculed him. Then he put them all out. He took along the child's father and mother and those who were with him and entered the room where the child was.
41  He took the child by the hand and said to her, "Talitha koum," which means, "Little girl, I say to you, arise!"
42  The girl, a child of twelve, arose immediately and walked around. (At that) they were utterly astounded.
43  He gave strict orders that no one should know this and said that she should be given something to eat.

*Our Father who art in Heaven, hallowed be thy name; Thy kingdom come Thy will be done on earth as it is in heaven. Give us this day our daily bread; and forgive us our trespasses as we forgive those who trespass against us; and lead us not into temptation but deliver us from evil. Amen*

*Repeat ten times:*

*Hail Mary, full of grace. The Lord is with thee. Blessed art thou amongst women, and blessed is the fruit of thy womb, Jesus.*
    *Holy Mary, Mother of God, pray for us sinners, now and at the hour of our death. Amen.*

*Glory be to the Father, and to the Son, and to the Holy Spirit, as it was in the beginning, is now, and ever shall be, world without end. Amen…*

*O my Jesus, forgive us our sins, save us from the fires of hell, and lead all souls to Heaven, especially those in most need of Your Mercy. Amen*

# Seventh Miracle Healing of Jesus

# Woman with Hemorrhage—Seventh Decade

## Mark 5:25–34; see Matthew 9:20–22 and Luke 8:43–48

25  There was a woman afflicted with hemorrhages for twelve years.
26  She had suffered greatly at the hands of many doctors and had spent all that she had. Yet she was not helped but only grew worse.
27  She had heard about Jesus and came up behind him in the crowd and touched his cloak.
28  She said, "If I but touch his clothes, I shall be cured."
29  Immediately her flow of blood dried up. She felt in her body that she was healed of her affliction.
30  Jesus, aware at once that power had gone out from him, turned around in the crowd and asked, "Who has touched my clothes?"

*Our Father who art in Heaven, hallowed be thy name; Thy kingdom come Thy will be done on earth as it is in heaven. Give us this day our daily bread.*

*And forgive us our trespasses as we forgive those who trespass against us; and lead us not into temptation but deliver us from evil. Amen*

*Repeat ten times:*

*Hail Mary, full of grace. The Lord is with thee. Blessed art thou amongst women, and blessed is the fruit of thy womb, Jesus.*

*Holy Mary, Mother of God, pray for us sinners, now and at the hour of our death. Amen.*

*Glory be to the Father, and to the Son, and to the Holy Spirit, as it was in the beginning, is now, and ever shall be, world without end. Amen.*

*O my Jesus, forgive us our sins, save us from the fires of hell, and lead all souls to Heaven, especially those in most need of Your Mercy. Amen*

# The River Jordan

ELIZABETH ANNE REEVES

# Eighth Miracle Healing of Jesus

# Woman's Daughter—Eighth Decade

## Matthew 15:21–28; see also Mark 7:24–30

21  Then Jesus went from that place and withdrew to the region of Tyre and Sidon.

22  And behold, a Canaanite woman of that district came (The woman was a Greek, a Syrophoenician by birth according to Mark) and called out, "Have pity on me, Lord, Son of David! My daughter is tormented by a demon."

23  But he did not say a word in answer to her. His disciples came and asked him, "Send her away, for she keeps calling out after us."

24  He said in reply, "I was sent only to the lost sheep of the house of Israel."

25  But the woman came and did him homage, saying, "Lord, help me."

26  He said in reply, "It is not right to take the food of the children" and throw it to the dogs."

27  She said, "Please, Lord, for even the dogs eat the scraps that fall from the table of their masters."

28  Then Jesus said to her in reply, "O woman, great is your faith!" Let it be done for you as you wish." And her daughter was healed from that hour.

*Our Father who art in Heaven, hallowed be thy name; Thy kingdom come Thy will be done on earth as it is in heaven. Give us this day our daily bread.*

*And forgive us our trespasses as we forgive those who trespass against us; and lead us not into temptation but deliver us from evil. Amen*

Repeat ten times:

*Hail Mary, full of grace. The Lord is with thee. Blessed art thou amongst women, and blessed is the fruit of thy womb, Jesus.*

*Holy Mary, Mother of God, pray for us sinners, now and at the hour of our death. Amen.*

*Glory be to the Father, and to the Son, and to the Holy Spirit, as it was in the beginning, is now, and ever shall be, world without end. Amen.*

*O my Jesus, forgive us our sins, save us from the fires of hell, and lead all souls to Heaven, especially those in most need of Your Mercy. Amen*

# Ninth Miracle Healing of Jesus

## Blind Man at Bethsaida—Ninth Decade

**Mark 8:22–26**

22  When they arrived at Bethsaida, they brought to him a blind man and begged him to touch him.
23  He took the blind man by the hand and led him outside the village. Putting spittle on his eyes he laid his hands on him and asked, "Do you see anything?"
24  Looking up he replied, "I see people looking like trees and walking."
25  Then he laid hands on his eyes a second time and he saw clearly; his sight was restored, and he could see everything distinctly.
26  Then he sent him home and said, "Do not even go into the village."

*Our Father who art in Heaven, hallowed be thy name; Thy kingdom come Thy will be done on earth as it is in heaven. Give us this day our daily bread.*

*And forgive us our trespasses as we forgive those who trespass against us; and lead us not into temptation but deliver us from evil. Amen*

*Repeat ten times:*

*Hail Mary, full of grace. The Lord is with thee. Blessed art thou amongst women, and blessed is the fruit of thy womb, Jesus.*

*Holy Mary, Mother of God, pray for us sinners, now and at the hour of our death. Amen*

*Glory be to the Father, and to the Son, and to the Holy Spirit, as it was in the beginning, is now, and ever shall be, world without end. Amen.*

*O my Jesus, forgive us our sins, save us from the fires of hell, and lead all souls to Heaven, especially those in most need of Your Mercy. Amen*

## The Pool of Bethsaida

HEALING SCRIPTURES

# Tenth Miracle Healing of Jesus

# Sick Man at the Pool of Bethsaida—Tenth Decade

## John 5:1–15

1   After this, there was a feast of the Jews, and Jesus went up to Jerusalem.
2   Now there is in Jerusalem at the Sheep [Gate] a pool called in Hebrew, Bethesda, with five porticoes.
3   In these lay a large number of ill, blind, lame, and crippled.
4   For [from time to time] an angel of the Lord used to come down into the pool; and the water was stirred up, so the first one to get in [after the stirring of the water] was healed of whatever disease afflicted him.
5   One man was there who had been ill for thirty-eight years.
6   When Jesus saw him lying there and knew that he had been ill for a long time, he said to him, "Do you want to be well?"
7   The sick man answered him, "Sir, I have no one to put me into the pool when the water is stirred up; while I am on my way, someone else gets down there before me."
8   Jesus said to him, "Rise, take up your mat, and walk."
9   Immediately the man became well, took up his mat, and walked. Now that day was a Sabbath.

*Our Father who art in Heaven, hallowed be thy name; Thy kingdom come Thy will be done on earth as it is in heaven. Give us this day our daily bread. And forgive us our trespasses as we forgive those who trespass against us; and lead us not into temptation but deliver us from evil. Amen*

*Repeat ten times:*

*Hail Mary, full of grace. The Lord is with thee. Blessed art thou amongst women, and blessed is the fruit of thy womb, Jesus.*
    *Holy Mary, Mother of God, pray for us sinners, now and at the hour of our death. Amen*

*Glory be to the Father, and to the Son, and to the Holy Spirit, as it was in the beginning, is now, and ever shall be, world without end. Amen…*

*O my Jesus, forgive us our sins, save us from the fires of hell, and lead all souls to Heaven, especially those in most need of Your Mercy. Amen*

# Eleventh Miracle Healing of Jesus

# Man Born Blind—Eleventh Decade

## John 9:1–7

1. As he passed by he saw a man blind from birth.
2. His disciples asked him, "Rabbi, who sinned, this man or his parents, that he was born blind?"
3. Jesus answered, "Neither he nor his parents sinned; it is so that the works of God might be made visible through him.
4. We have to do the works of the one who sent me while it is day. Night is coming when no one can work.
5. While I am in the world, I am the light of the world."
6. When he had said this, he spat on the ground and made clay with the saliva, and smeared the clay on his eyes,
7. And said to him, "Go wash in the Pool of Siloam" (which means Sent). So he went and washed, and came back able to see.

*Our Father who art in Heaven, hallowed be thy name; Thy kingdom come Thy will be done on earth as it is in heaven. Give us this day our daily bread. And forgive us our trespasses as we forgive those who trespass against us; and lead us not into temptation but deliver us from evil. Amen*

*Repeat ten times:*

*Hail Mary, full of grace. The Lord is with thee. Blessed art thou amongst women, and blessed is the fruit of thy womb, Jesus.*
    *Holy Mary, Mother of God, pray for us sinners, now and at the hour of our death. Amen.*

*Glory be to the Father, and to the Son, and to the Holy Spirit, as it was in the beginning, is now, and ever shall be, world without end. Amen.*

*O my Jesus, forgive us our sins, save us from the fires of hell, and lead all souls to Heaven, especially those in most need of Your Mercy. Amen*

# Twelfth Miracle Healing of Jesus

## Crippled Woman—Twelfth Decade

### Luke 13:10–17

10 He was teaching in a synagogue on the Sabbath.

11 And a woman was there who for eighteen years had been crippled by a spirit; she was bent over, completely incapable of standing erect.

12 When Jesus saw her, he called to her and said, "Woman, you are set free of your infirmity."

13 He laid his hands on her, and she at once stood up straight and glorified God.

14 But the leader of the synagogue, indignant that Jesus had cured on the Sabbath, said to the crowd in reply, "There are six days when work should be done. Come on those days to be cured, not on the Sabbath day."

15 The Lord said to him in reply, "Hypocrites! Does not each one of you on the Sabbath untie his ox or his ass from the manger and lead it out for watering?

16 This daughter of Abraham, whom Satan has bound for eighteen years now, ought she not to have been set free on the Sabbath day from this bondage?"

17 When he said this, all his adversaries were humiliated; and the whole crowd rejoiced at all the splendid deeds done by him.

*Our Father who art in Heaven, hallowed be thy name; Thy kingdom come Thy will be done on earth as it is in heaven. Give us this day our daily bread. And forgive us our trespasses as we forgive those who trespass against us; and lead us not into temptation but deliver us from evil. Amen*

*Repeat ten times:*

*Hail Mary, full of grace. The Lord is with thee. Blessed art thou amongst women, and blessed is the fruit of thy womb, Jesus.*

*Holy Mary, Mother of God, pray for us sinners, now and at the hour of our death. Amen.*

*Glory be to the Father, and to the Son, and to the Holy Spirit, as it was in the beginning, is now, and ever shall be, world without end. Amen.*

*O my Jesus, forgive us our sins, save us from the fires of hell, and lead all souls to Heaven, especially those in most need of Your Mercy. Amen*

# The Pool of Siloam

# Thirteenth Miracle Healing of Jesus

# Man with Edema—Thirteenth Decade

## Luke 14:1–4

1. On a Sabbath he went to dine at the home of one of the leading Pharisees, and the people there were observing him carefully.
2. In front of him there was a man suffering from dropsy (edema).
3. Jesus spoke to the scholars of the law and Pharisees in reply, asking, "Is it lawful to cure on the Sabbath or not?"
4. But they kept silent; so he took the man and, after he had healed him, dismissed him.
5. Then he said to them, "Who among you, if your son or ox falls into a cistern, would not immediately pull him out on the Sabbath day?"
6. But they were unable to answer his question.

*Our Father who art in Heaven, hallowed be thy name; Thy kingdom come Thy will be done on earth as it is in heaven. Give us this day our daily bread. And forgive us our trespasses as we forgive those who trespass against us; and lead us not into temptation but deliver us from evil. Amen*

*Repeat ten times:*

*Hail Mary, full of grace. The Lord is with thee. Blessed art thou amongst women, and blessed is the fruit of thy womb, Jesus.*
    *Holy Mary, Mother of God, pray for us sinners, now and at the hour of our death. Amen*

*Glory be to the Father, and to the Son, and to the Holy Spirit, as it was in the beginning, is now, and ever shall be, world without end. Amen.*

*O my Jesus, forgive us our sins, save us from the fires of hell, and lead all souls to Heaven, especially those in most need of Your Mercy. Amen*

# Fourteenth Miracle Healing of Jesus

# Ten Men with Leprosy—Fourteenth Decade

## Luke 17:11–19

11  As he continued his journey to Jerusalem, he traveled through Samaria and Galilee
12  As he was entering a village, ten lepers met [him]. They stood at a distance from him
13  And raised their voice, saying, "Jesus, Master! Have pity on us!"
14  And when he saw them, he said, "Go show yourselves to the priests." As they were going, they were cleansed.
15  And one of them, realizing he had been healed, returned, glorifying God in a loud voice.
16  And he fell at the feet of Jesus and thanked him. He was a Samaritan.
17  Jesus said in reply, "Ten were cleansed, were they not? Where are the other nine?
18  Has none but this foreigner returned to give thanks to God?"
19  Then he said to him, "Stand up and go; your faith has saved you."

*Our Father who art in Heaven, hallowed be thy name; Thy kingdom come Thy will be done on earth as it is in heaven. Give us this day our daily bread. And forgive us our trespasses as we forgive those who trespass against us; and lead us not into temptation but deliver us from evil. Amen*

*Repeat ten times:*

*Hail Mary, full of grace. The Lord is with thee. Blessed art thou amongst women, and blessed is the fruit of thy womb, Jesus.*
    *Holy Mary, Mother of God, pray for us sinners, now and at the hour of our death. Amen*

*Glory be to the Father, and to the Son, and to the Holy Spirit, as it was in the beginning, is now, and ever shall be, world without end. Amen.*

*O my Jesus, forgive us our sins, save us from the fires of hell, and lead all souls to Heaven, especially those in most need of Your Mercy. Amen*

# Fifteenth Miracle Healing of Jesus

## Bartimaeus—Fifteenth Decade

**Mark 10:46–52**

46 They came to Jericho. And as he was leaving Jericho with his disciples and a sizable crowd, Bartimaeus, a blind man, the son of Timaeus, sat by the roadside begging.

47 On hearing that it was Jesus of Nazareth, he began to cry out and say, "Jesus, son of David, have pity on me."

48 And many rebuked him, telling him to be silent. But he kept calling out all the more, "Son of David, have pity on me."

49 Jesus stopped and said, "Call him." So they called the blind man, saying to him, "Take courage; get up, he is calling you."

50 He threw aside his cloak, sprang up, and came to Jesus.

51 Jesus said to him in reply, "What do you want me to do for you?" The blind man replied to him, "Master, I want to see."

52 Jesus told him, "Go your way; your faith has saved you." Immediately he received his sight and followed him on the way.

*Our Father who art in Heaven, hallowed be thy name; Thy kingdom come Thy will be done on earth as it is in heaven. Give us this day our daily bread. And forgive us our trespasses as we forgive those who trespass against us; and lead us not into temptation but deliver us from evil. Amen*

*Repeat ten times:*

*Hail Mary, full of grace. The Lord is with thee. Blessed art thou amongst women, and blessed is the fruit of thy womb, Jesus.*

*Holy Mary, Mother of God, pray for us sinners, now and at the hour of our death. Amen*

*Glory be to the Father, and to the Son, and to the Holy Spirit, as it was in the beginning, is now, and ever shall be, world without end. Amen.*

*O my Jesus, forgive us our sins, save us from the fires of hell, and lead all souls to Heaven, especially those in most need of Your Mercy. Amen*

# Sixteenth Miracle Healing of Jesus

# The Man with a Withered Hand—Sixteenth Decade

## Matthew 12:9–16

9   Moving on from there, he went into their synagogue.

10  And behold, there was a man there who had a withered hand. They questioned him, "Is it lawful to cure on the Sabbath? So that they might accuse him.

11  He said to them, "Which one of you who has a sheep that falls into a pit on the Sabbath will not take hold of it and lift it out?

12  How much more valuable a person is than a sheep. So it is lawful to do good on the Sabbath."

13  Then he said to the man, "Stretch out your hand." He stretched it out, and it was restored as sound as the other.

14  But the Pharisees went out and took counsel against him to put him to death.

*Our Father who art in Heaven, hallowed be thy name; Thy kingdom come Thy will be done on earth as it is in heaven. Give us this day our daily bread. And forgive us our trespasses as we forgive those who trespass against us; and lead us not into temptation but deliver us from evil. Amen*

*Repeat ten times:*

*Hail Mary, full of grace. The Lord is with thee. Blessed art thou amongst women, and blessed is the fruit of thy womb, Jesus.*
    *Holy Mary, Mother of God, pray for us sinners, now and at the hour of our death. Amen.*

*Glory be to the Father, and to the Son, and to the Holy Spirit, as it was in the beginning, is now, and ever shall be, world without end. Amen.*

*O my Jesus, forgive us our sins, save us from the fires of hell, and lead all souls to Heaven, especially those in most need of Your Mercy. Amen*

# Seventeenth Miracle Healing of Jesus

# The Healing of Two Blind Men—Seventeenth Decade

## Matthew 9:27–31

27 As Jesus went on from there, two blind men followed Him, crying out, "Have mercy on us, Son of David!"

28 When He entered the house, the blind men came up to Him, and Jesus *said to them, "Do you believe that I am able to do this?" They *said to Him, "Yes, Lord."

29 Then He touched their eyes, saying, "It shall be done to you according to your faith."

30 And their eyes were opened. And Jesus sternly warned them: "See that no one knows about this!"

31 But they went out and spread the news about Him throughout all that land.

# The Healing of Two Blind Men

**Matthew 20:29–34**

29  As they left Jericho, a great crowd followed him.
30  Two blind men were sitting by the roadside, and when they heard that Jesus was passing by, they cried out, "[Lord,] Son of David, have pity on us!"
31  The crowd warned them to be silent, but they called out all the more, Lord, Son of David, have pity on us!"
32  Jesus stopped and called them and said, "What do you want me to do for you?"
33  They answered him, "Lord, let our eyes be opened."
34  Moved with pity, Jesus touched their eyes. Immediately they received their sight, and followed him.

*Our Father who art in Heaven, hallowed be thy name; Thy kingdom come Thy will be done on earth as it is in heaven. Give us this day our daily bread. And forgive us our trespasses as we forgive those who trespass against us; and lead us not Into temptation but deliver us from evil. Amen*

*Repeat ten times:*

*Hail Mary, full of grace. The Lord is with thee. Blessed art thou amongst women, and blessed is the fruit of thy womb, Jesus.*
    *Holy Mary, Mother of God, pray for us sinners, now and at the hour of our death. Amen.*

*Glory be to the Father, and to the Son, and to the Holy Spirit, as it was in the beginning, is now, and ever shall be, world without end. Amen.*

*O my Jesus, forgive us our sins, save us from the fires of hell, and lead all souls to Heaven, especially those in most need of Your Mercy. Amen*

# Eighteenth Miracle Healing of Jesus

# The Healing of the Blind Beggar—Eighteenth Decade

## Luke 18:35–43

32  Now as he approached Jericho a blind man was sitting by the roadside begging,
33  And hearing a crowd going by, he inquired what was happening.
34  They told him, "Jesus of Nazareth is passing by."
35  He shouted, "Jesus, Son of David,* have pity on me!"
36  The people walking in front rebuked him, telling him to be silent, but he kept calling out all the more, "Son of David, have pity on me!"
37  Then Jesus stopped and ordered that he be brought to him; and when he came near, Jesus asked him,
38  "What do you want me to do for you?" He replied, "Lord, please let me see."
39  Jesus told him, "Have sight; your faith has saved you."
40  He immediately received his sight and followed him, giving glory to God. When they saw this, all the people gave praise to God.

*Our Father who art in Heaven, hallowed be thy name; Thy kingdom come Thy will be done on earth as it is in heaven. Give us this day our daily bread. And forgive us our trespasses as we forgive those who trespass against us; and lead us not into temptation but deliver us from evil. Amen*

*Repeat ten times:*

*Hail Mary, full of grace. The Lord is with thee. Blessed art thou amongst women, and blessed is the fruit of thy womb, Jesus.*

*Holy Mary, Mother of God, pray for us sinners, now and at the hour of our death. Amen.*

*Glory be to the Father, and to the Son, and to the Holy Spirit, as it was in the beginning, is now, and ever shall be, world without end. Amen.*

*O my Jesus, forgive us our sins, save us from the fires of hell, and lead all souls to Heaven, especially those in most need of Your Mercy. Amen*

# Nineteenth Miracle Healing of Jesus

# Healing of the Ear of Malchus—Nineteenth Decade

## Mark 14: 47–53

47 While he was still speaking, a crowd approached and in front was one of the Twelve, a man named Judas. He went up to Jesus to kiss him.

48 Jesus said to him, "Judas, are you betraying the Son of Man with a kiss?"

49 His disciples realized what was about to happen, and they asked, "Lord, shall we strike with a sword?"

50 And one of them struck the high priest's servant and cut off his right ear.

51 But Jesus said in reply, "Stop, no more of this!" Then he touched the servant's ear and healed him.

52 And Jesus said to the chief priests and temple guards and elders who had come for him, "Have you come out as against a robber, with swords and clubs?

53 Day after day I was with you in the temple area, and you did not seize me; but this is your hour, the time for the power of darkness."

# Church of the Holy Sepulcher

*Our Father who art in Heaven, hallowed be thy name; Thy kingdom come Thy will be done on earth as it is in heaven. Give us this day our daily bread. And forgive us our trespasses as we forgive those who trespass against us; and lead us not into temptation but deliver us from evil. Amen*

*Repeat ten times:*

*Hail Mary, full of grace. The Lord is with thee. Blessed art thou amongst women, and blessed is the fruit of thy womb, Jesus.*
    *Holy Mary, Mother of God, pray for us sinners, now and at the hour of our death. Amen.*

*Glory be to the Father, and to the Son, and to the Holy Spirit, as it was in the beginning, is now, and ever shall be, world without end. Amen.*

*O my Jesus, forgive us our sins, save us from the fires of hell, and lead all souls to Heaven, especially those in most need of Your Mercy. Amen*

# Twentieth Miracle Healing of Jesus

# Raising the Dead

## 1. Raising the Widow's Son at Nain—Twentieth Decade

### Luke 7:11–17

11  Soon afterward he journeyed to a city called Nain, and his disciples and a large crowd accompanied him.

12  As he drew near to the gate of the city, a man who had died was being carried out, the only son of his mother, and she was a widow. A large crowd from the city was with her.

13  When the Lord saw her, he was moved with pity for her and said to her, "Do not weep."

14  He stepped forward and touched the coffin; at this the bearers halted, and he said, "Young man, I tell you, arise!"

15  The dead man sat up and began to speak, and Jesus gave him to his mother.

16  Fear seized them all, and they glorified God, exclaiming, "A great prophet has arisen in our midst," and "God has visited his people."

17  This report about him spread through the whole of Judea and in all the surrounding region

## 2. Raising Lazarus from the Dead

### John 11:32–44

32   When Mary came to where Jesus was and saw him, she fell at his feet and said to him, "Lord, if you had been here, my brother would not have died."

33   When Jesus saw her weeping and the Jews who had come with her weeping, he became perturbed and deeply troubled,

34   And said, "Where have you laid him?" They said to him, "Sir, come and see."

35   And Jesus wept.

36   So the Jews said, "See how he loved him."

37   But some of them said, "Could not the one who opened the eyes of the blind man have done something so that this man would not have died?"

38   So Jesus, perturbed again, came to the tomb. It was a cave, and a stone lay across it.

39   Jesus said, "Take away the stone." Martha, the dead man's sister, said to him, "Lord, by now there will be a stench; he has been dead for four days."

40   Jesus said to her, "Did I not tell you that if you believe you will see the glory of God?"

41   So they took away the stone. And Jesus raised his eyes and said, "Father, I thank you for hearing me.

42   I know that you always hear me; but because of the crowd here I have said this, that they may believe that you sent me."

43   And when he had said this, he cried out in a loud voice, "Lazarus, come out!"

44   The dead man came out, tied hand and foot with burial bands, and his face was wrapped in a cloth. So Jesus said to them, "Untie him and let him go."

*Our Father who art in Heaven, hallowed be thy name; Thy kingdom come Thy will be done on earth as it is in heaven. Give us this day our daily bread. And forgive us our trespasses as we forgive those who trespass against us; and lead us not into temptation but deliver us from evil. Amen*

*Repeat ten times:*

*Hail Mary, full of grace. The Lord is with thee. Blessed art thou amongst women, and blessed is the fruit of thy womb, Jesus.*
   *Holy Mary, Mother of God, pray for us sinners, now and at the hour of our death. Amen.*

*Glory be to the Father, and to the Son, and to the Holy Spirit, as it was in the beginning, is now, and ever shall be, world without end. Amen.*

*O my Jesus, forgive us our sins, save us from the fires of hell, and lead all souls to Heaven, especially those in most need of Your Mercy. Amen*

### Hail Holy Queen

**Hail, Holy Queen, Mother of Mercy, our life, our sweetness and our hope! To thee do we cry, poor banished children of Eve. To thee do we send up our sighs, mourning and weeping in this valley of tears! Turn, then, O most gracious Advocate, thine eyes of mercy toward us, and after this, our exile, show unto us the blessed Fruit of thy womb, Jesus. O clement, O loving, O sweet Virgin Mary.**

*V. Pray for us, O holy Mother of God.*
*R. That we may be made worthy of the promises of Christ.*

## Mount of Temptation in the Jericho Wilderness

# Author's Commentary

**You Have Prayed. Now What Do You Do?**
**© Elizabeth Anne Reeves 2021**

**NOTE:** This portion of *Healing Rosary* is not subject to the Archdiocese of Washington *Imprimatur* and *Obstat*. The views in this author's commentary are strictly the opinions of the author and the product of her personal experiences.

After half an hour of praying, how do spend the rest of your day? I suggest you spend time:

1. affirming your faith in God,
2. believing Jesus came to heal you,
3. forgiving those who hurt you,
4. searching scriptures, and
5. loving generously.

Proverbs 4:20–22 tells us we need to listen to God's words, to not let them depart from our eyes, and to keep them in our hearts. His words are life to those of us who find them, and they bring health to our bodies. According to Psalm 91:16, God's promise is long life to His people.

The three Charismatic Catholic priests whom I called friends told me that if our spirits, the eternal parts of us, are healed, our minds and bodies will follow. The Lord is more concerned with our eternal spirits. Jesus says he is the way and the truth and the life. No one comes to the Father except through him (John 14:6).

Some lost their way in a barren desert; found no path toward a city to live in…Some lived in darkness and gloom, imprisoned in misery and chains…Some fell sick from their wicked ways, afflicted because of their sins...Some went off to sea in ships...on the deep water...and [were] tossed [by] the waves on high. They rose up to the heavens, sank to the depths; their hearts trembled in fear...their skill was of no avail. (Psalm 107:4, 10, 17, 23, and 25–27)

God changed rivers into desert, springs of water into thirsty ground...because of the wickedness of the people...He poured out contempt on princes, made them wander trackless wastes, [w]here they were diminished and brought low through misery and cruel oppression. (Psalm 107:33, 34, 39, and 40)

But Psalm 107:19–20 says "In their distress, they cried to the Lord, who saved them in their peril, sent forth his word to heal them and snatched them from the grave."

The answers to the human cry for healing can be found in the words of our Lord in the Holy Scriptures. Have you lost your way in life? Are you depressed? Are you sick because of your sins? Are you in fear of forces beyond your control? Is life difficult because of your choices in life? Have you been cruel to people and suffered the consequences?

How do we start the healing process in our spirits and access that balm in Gilead?[1]

> There was a Pharisee named Nicodemus who asked Jesus a similar question. Jesus answered that unless a person is born again, he or she cannot see the kingdom of God (John 3:3).

---

[1] This is a reference to Jeremiah 8:22: "Is there no balm in Gilead, no healer here?" The balm of Gilead was a rare perfume used medicinally as an antioxidant, anti-inflammatory, antiseptic, and diuretic. It is a term found in the Tyndale Bible of 1611. It is also figure of speech for a universal cure. In the lyrics of an old spiritual, it is used to signify salvation in Jesus: "Jesus can heal the sin-sick soul. / Jesus is the balm in Gilead."

Jesus also said what is born of the flesh is flesh, and what is born of the Spirit is spirit (John 3:6). Clearly we are given spiritual lives beyond our mortal bodies at baptism.

Why is being born again important to healing? Both deliverance from sin and healing from all our afflictions is found in the atonement of Christ. In Paul's letter to the Galatians 3:13, he wrote that as the bronze serpent was lifted, it removed the Israelites' curse; so too our curse is removed by the lifting up of Christ. In the Gospel of John 1:13, Jesus clearly states that he descends from God. No human has or will ascend to God unless Jesus is lifted like Moses lifted the bronze serpent up in the wilderness. Jesus, by referencing the bronze serpent in the wilderness, conveyed to the apostles and disciples that he was God's Messiah, and that God's people would be healed through his death on the cross.

In the Old Testament, Numbers 21:4–9 talks about the bronze serpent. The Israelites' patience was worn out by traveling. People complained against God and Moses, asking, "Why have you brought us up from Egypt to die in the wilderness, where there is no food or water?" Poisonous snakes bit many Israelites, and many died. The people came to Moses and said, "We have sinned in complaining against the LORD and you. Pray to the LORD to take the serpents from us." Moses prayed for his people, and the Lord said to Moses, "Make an image of a snake and mount it on a pole, and everyone who has been bitten will look at it and recover." Moses made a bronze serpent and mounted it on a pole, and whenever a serpent bit someone, the person looked at the bronze serpent and recovered.

Another Old Testament passage on healing to review in these days of coronavirus is Numbers 17:11–13.

Then Moses said to Aaron, "Take your censer, put fire from the altar in it, lay incense on it, and bring it quickly to the community to make atonement for them; for wrath has come forth from the LORD and the plague has begun." Aaron took his censer just as Moses directed and ran in among the assembly, where the plague had already begun among the people. Then he offered the incense and made atonement for the people, while standing there between the living and the dead. And so, the scourge was stopped.

Aaron, as priest, made a sacrificial atonement on the altar for the people to be healed of their illness. So too Jesus Christ, our great high priest, by his atonement on the cross has delivered us from the pandemic of sin and sickness. Every time you see the crucifix lifted high in a Catholic church, remember Jesus said he must be lifted like Moses lifted the bronze serpent in the wilderness for us to ascend to heaven and to be healed of our afflictions. In John 3:13–15 Jesus says to Nicodemus, "No one has gone up to heaven except the one who has come down from heaven, the Son of Man. And just as Moses lifted up the serpent in the desert, so must the Son of Man be lifted up, so that everyone who believes in him may have eternal life."

As faithful servants of God, we need to stop complaining and start praising God for the blessings we have had in our lives. An attitude of gratitude is a double blessing to you and to those around you.

"Yet you, the Holy One, who make your home in the praises of Israel" (Psalm 22:3) is sometimes translated to read God "inhabits" the praises of His people. The Hebrew word *ysb* is translated "enthroned," conveying the idea of possession and control.

Praising God opens the door to receiving God's healing power. It is the opposite of the complaining and murmuring against God that got the Israelites in trouble spiritually. Complaining and displaying constant negativity toward God and their circumstances caused sickness and death among the Israelites. We need to instead express faith in our thoughts, our prayers, and in our daily lives.

Since you are not Nicodemus with Jesus 2,000 years ago, how can you be born again? The best example is the good thief's discourse with Jesus at Calvary. Tradition calls the good thief St. Dismas. Read the passage in the Gospel of Luke 23:39–43 for direction in prayer.

One of the criminals hanging there abused him: "Are you not the Christ? Save yourself and us as well." But the other spoke up and rebuked him. "Have you no fear of God at all?" he said. "You got the same sentence as he did, but in our case we deserved it: we are paying for what we did. But this man has done nothing wrong." Then he said, "Jesus, remember me when you come into your kingdom." He answered him, "In truth I tell you, today you will be with me in paradise."

This passage I recommend as a formula for being born again because we know from Jesus's own words that the good thief made it to heaven.

1. St. Dismas gave Jesus honor or worship when he asked the other thief, "do you not fear God?" He recognized Jesus as the Lord, the Messiah, first.
2. The good thief then acknowledged he was a sinner and was sorry for his sins. He felt he deserved to die for those sins.
3. The good thief saw also the goodness of Jesus and trusted in his mercy enough to ask to go to Jesus's kingdom with him after death. Jesus saw the good thief's repentance and his faith in him. Our beloved savior responded in his mercy to promise heaven to St. Dismas. By extension, Jesus in his mercy and faithfulness promises us paradise too if we repent and turn to him for mercy and grace.

How do we access healing in Christ's atonement after we are born again? Jesus said he would send another we call the Holy Spirit. Jesus in 1 John 2:1 is our advocate. The Greek legal term for advocate means defense attorney. The Holy Spirit as advocate is a teacher, a witness to Jesus, and a prosecutor of the world in John 14:16.

> But to each one is given the manifestation of the Spirit for the common good. For to one is given the word of wisdom through the Spirit, and to another the word of knowledge according to the same Spirit; to another faith by the same Spirit, and to another gifts of healing by the one Spirit, and to another

the effecting of miracles, and to another prophecy, and to another the distinguishing of spirits, to another *various* kinds of tongues, and to another the interpretation of tongues. (1 Corinthians 12: 7–10)

Healing is a gift from the Holy Spirit.

How do we receive the Holy Spirit? At baptism, the Holy Spirit rested on Jesus, according to scriptures. The Holy Spirit fell on the early church in the second chapter of Acts when the disciples gathered together in one accord.

But how do you receive these gifts of the Holy Spirit? Luke 11:13 reads, "If you then, who are wicked, know how to give good gifts to your children, how much more will the Father in heaven give the Holy Spirit to those who ask him?"

I direct the reader to Gospel of John 4:7–42 to portions of the story of the woman at the well.

> A woman of Samaria came to draw water. Jesus said to her, "Give me a drink." The Samaritan woman said to him, "How can you, a Jew, ask me, a Samaritan woman, for a drink?" (For Jews use nothing in common with Samaritans.) Jesus answered and said to her, "If you knew the gift of God and who is saying to you, 'Give me a drink,' you would have asked him, and he would have given you living water." Jesus answered and said to her, "Everyone who drinks this water will be thirsty again; but whoever drinks the water I shall give will never thirst; the water I shall give will become in him a spring of water welling up to eternal life." The woman said to him, "Sir, give me this water, so that I may not be thirsty or have to keep coming here to draw water." But the hour is coming, and is now here, when true worshipers will worship the

> Father in Spirit and truth; and indeed, the Father seeks such people to worship him. God is Spirit, and those who worship him must worship in Spirit and truth.

Simply put, we are more than just physical bodies or brains within our bodies. We have spirits created in the image of God. They are our emotional hearts, our consciences which differentiate between good and evil. That spirit is neglected today in our culture. It is what we will take to heaven with us when we die. What is the composition of this spirit of God in us?

> These three things remain, Faith Hope and Love with Love being the greatness of all. (1 Corinthians 13:13)

So what heals us spiritually? It is God's love. You need love to be healed so that is why forgiveness is important. Forgive others and forgive yourself. It is included in the Lord's Prayer as a precondition to forgiveness of sins. We cannot love or receive love without forgiveness in our hearts.

# Testimonies and Practical Guide

Studies have shown that people who are prayed for recover faster than those who are not. Those who did not know people prayed for them recovered faster too. There is something more than coincidence to prayer.

I would use this scriptural rosary and insert the names of your loved ones in the scripture. For example, John 4:46 could be read as follows: "Jesus said to [me], 'You may go; [name of your child or spouse, friend or relative] will live.' [I] believed what Jesus said to [me] and left."

The enemy of faith is fear. Job said of his calamities, "For what I feared overtakes me: what I dreaded comes upon me. I have no peace nor ease, for trouble has come" (Job 3:25).

The Lord healed me of cancer three times. Extraordinarily little is as scary as the dreaded C word. But Jesus died on the cross so by His stripes you and I were and are healed (Isaiah 53:5 and 1 Peter 2:24). When fear arose in my heart, I recited scriptures on healing, claimed I was healed, and told myself I would not receive cancer in my body. And my three priests and a Charismatic pastor prayed for me.

The first time, the first doctor thought I had uterine cancer or at least endometriosis. After the surgery, he looked like a ghost and said he found nothing. I was happy even though he looked spooked.

The second time, the second doctor thought I had cervical cancer from a Pap smear result of Class III. He performed a cervical freezing. The second Pap smear came back Class II. I said it was only an infection because of the cervical freezing. The second doctor wanted to use Interferon. I said no and that I wanted another opinion. I went to a third specialist, a reproductive gynecologist and surgeon and one of only three in the country at that time. The Pap smear and biopsy came back Class I. It was normal! Of course,

Doctor No. 3 said I probably never had it. Doctor No. 2 put in my permanent medical record that I had chronic cervicitis. I stayed with Doctor No. 3 and never had cervicitis.

The third time, at forty-two years-old, my left ovary was four times the normal size and there was a cyst the size of a grapefruit on it. This was significant because when my mother was forty-two, she had a cyst the size of a grapefruit on her left ovary. She had ovarian cancer and died eighteen months later. Ovarian cancer is 50 percent more likely in women whose mothers had it. Even Doctor No. 3 was worried. I had the ovary and cyst removed. The pathology report said that the ovary was normal and the cyst benign.

Doctor No. 3 apologized for removing normal tissue; he was sure it was cancer. I told him either God healed it, or he caught it before it metastasized. Either way, I was glad it was gone.

All three times, my three priests, my Charismatic pastor, and many others prayed for me. Faith in numbers helps too for prayer support. I listen to contemporary Christian radio in the car and at home to stay in a positive and worshipful attitude. I cannot say why some people have spontaneous healing, some are healed over time, some get better, and some have no change. I only know I have found that prayer works for me. I believe Christ Jesus our Lord healed people during his time on Earth. He is the same yesterday, today, and forever. Christ is no respecter of persons and what He did for me, a sinner, He also wants to do for you.

# 24 Glory Be Novena to St. Therese The Little Flower

For nine days recite the **"Glory be to the Father" twenty-four times a day** asking the Holy Trinity for the favors and graces like showered on Saint Therese The Little Flower during the twenty-four years of her life on earth.

The priest who authored this prayer asked Saint Therese, that as a sign that his novena was heard he would receive from someone a rose.

On the third day of the first **24 Glory Be Novena**, an unknown person sought out the first priest who prayed the first **St Theresa Novena** and presented him with a beautiful rose. Roses are a sign of answered prayer from heaven.

Glory Be to the Father, and to the Son, and to the Holy Spirit.
As it was in the beginning, is now, and ever shall be.
(24 times a day for 9 days.)

# Augustine's Bedtime Prayer

**Evening Prayer of St Augustine**
(354-430 CE)

Watch, O Lord, with those who wake, or watch, or weep tonight,
and give Your Angels and Saints charge over those who sleep.
Tend Your sick ones, O Lord Christ.
Rest Your weary ones.
Bless Your dying ones.
Soothe Your suffering ones.
Pity Your afflicted ones.
Shield Your joyous ones.
And all for Your love's sake.

Amen.

# Efficacious Novena to the Sacred Heart of Jesus

> This novena prayer was recited every day by Padre Pio for all those who asked for prayers.

I. **O my Jesus, you have said:** "Truly I say to you, ask and it will be given you, seek and you will find, knock and it will be opened to you." Behold I knock, I seek and ask for the grace of *[insert your intention.]* Our Father…Hail Mary…Glory be to the Father…Sacred Heart of Jesus, I place all my trust in you.

II. **O my Jesus, you have said:** "Truly I say to you, if you ask any thing of the Father in my name, He will give it to you." Behold, in your name, I ask the Father for the grace of *[insert your intention.]* Our Father…Hail Mary…Glory be to the Father…Sacred Heart of Jesus, I place all my trust in you.

III. **O my Jesus, you have said:** "Truly I say to you, heaven and earth will pass away but my words will not pass away." Encouraged by your infallible words I now ask for the grace of *[insert your intention.]* Our Father…Hail Mary…Glory be to the Father…Sacred Heart of Jesus, I place all my trust in you.

**O Sacred Heart of Jesus,** for whom it is impossible not to have compassion on the afflicted, have pity on us miserable sinners and grant us the grace which we ask of you, through the Sorrowful and Immaculate Heart of Mary, your tender mother and ours.

"**Hail, holy Queen,** Mother of mercy, hail, our life, our sweetness and our hope. To thee do we cry, poor banished children of Eve:

to thee do we send up our sighs, mourning and weeping in this vale of tears. Turn then, most gracious Advocate, thine eyes of mercy toward us, and after this our exile, show unto us the blessed fruit of thy womb, Jesus, O merciful, O loving, O sweet Virgin Mary!

# Novena to Saint Jude and the Sacred Heart of Jesus

This short novena to Saint Jude and the Sacred Heart of Jesus is prayed nine times per day (all at once or spread throughout the day) for nine days. The answer is expected by the eighth day. Publication of an answered prayer is expected.

The thanksgiving for the answer to prayer is then published—an act which can be as simple as sending it to your friends by e-mail or posting it in an online forum, placing an ad in the classified section of a newspaper or on the back of your church bulletin, or printing up copies to leave at your parish church.

> *May the Sacred Heart of Jesus be adored, glorified, loved, and preserved throughout the world, now and forever.*
>
> *Sacred Heart of Jesus, have mercy on us.*
>
> *St. Jude, worker of miracles, pray for us.*
>
> *St. Jude, help for the hopeless, pray for us.*

## Prayer to our Guardian Angel.

Angel of God. Angel of God, my guardian dear; to whom God's love commits me here, ever this day be at my side, to light, to guard, to rule and guide. Amen

# PSALM 23

USCCB

The LORD is my shepherd;
there is nothing I lack.

2 In green pastures he makes me lie down;
to still waters he leads me;
3 He restores my soul.
He guides me along right paths
for the sake of his name.
4 Even though I walk through the valley of the shadow of death,
I will fear no evil, for you are with me;
your rod and your staff comfort me.
5 You set a table before me
in front of my enemies;
You anoint my head with oil;
my cup overflows.

6 Indeed, goodness and mercy* will pursue me
all the days of my life;
I will dwell in the house of the LORD[f]
for endless days.

# Saint John Henry Newman

**(1801-1890)**
**A Daily Prayer**
May He support us all the day long,
till the shades lengthen and the evening comes,
and the busy world is hushed,
and the fever of life is over,
 and our work is done.
Then in His mercy may He give us a safe lodging,
and a holy rest and peace at the last.

**Saint Michael the Archangel,** defend us in battle; be our protection against the wickedness and snares of the devil. May God rebuke him, we humbly pray; and do thou, O Prince of the heavenly host, by the power of God, thrust into hell Satan and all the evil spirits who prowl about the world seeking the ruin of souls. **Amen.**

# The 15 Promises of the Virgin Mary to Those Who Pray the Rosary

*The Blessed Virgin Mary made these promises to Saint Dominic and to all who follow that "Whatever you ask in the Rosary will be granted."*

1. Whoever shall faithfully serve me by the recitation of the Rosary, shall receive signal graces.
2. I promise my special protection and the greatest graces to all those who shall recite the Rosary.
3. The Rosary shall be a powerful armor against hell, it will destroy vice, decrease sin, and defeat heresies.
4. The Rosary will cause virtue and good works to flourish; it will obtain for souls the abundant mercy of God; it will withdraw the hearts of men from the love of the world and its vanities, and will lift them to the desire for eternal things. Oh, that souls would sanctify themselves by this means.
5. The soul which recommends itself to me by the recitation of the Rosary, shall not perish.
6. Whoever shall recite the Rosary devoutly, applying himself to the consideration of its sacred mysteries shall never be conquered by misfortune. God will not chastise him in His justice, he shall not perish by an unprovided death; if he be just he shall remain in the grace of God, and become worthy of eternal life.
7. Whoever shall have a true devotion for the Rosary shall not die without the sacraments of the Church.
8. Those who are faithful to recite the Rosary shall have during their life and at their death the light of God and the plentitude of His graces; at the moment of death they shall participate in the merits of the saints in paradise.
9. I shall deliver from Purgatory those who have been devoted to the Rosary.

10. The faithful children of the Rosary shall merit a high degree of glory in Heaven.
11. You shall obtain all you ask of me by the recitation of the Rosary.
12. All those who propagate the Holy Rosary shall be aided by me in their necessities.
13. I have obtained from my Divine Son that all the advocates of the Rosary shall have for intercessors the entire celestial court during their life and at the hour of death.
14. All who recite the Rosary are my sons and daughters, and brothers and sisters of my only Son Jesus Christ.
15. Devotion of my Rosary is a great sign of predestination.

# The Magnificat

The Prayer of Mary

My soul proclaims the greatness of the Lord,
my spirit rejoices in God my Savior
for he has looked with favor on his lowly servant.
From this day all generations will call me blessed:
the Almighty has done great things for me,
and holy is his Name.

He has mercy on those who fear him
in every generation.
He has shown the strength of his arm,
he has scattered the proud in their conceit.

He has cast down the mighty from their thrones,
and has lifted up the lowly.
He has filled the hungry with good things,
and the rich he has sent away empty.

He has come to the help of his servant Israel
for he remembered his promise of mercy,
the promise he made to our fathers,
to Abraham and his children forever.x

# Miracle_Prayers

Heals all diseases
Psalms 103:3-5
Miracle Prayer that never fails:

I accept you as my Lord, God & Saviour. Heal me, change me, strengthen me, my body, soul & spirit. Come Lord Jesus, cover me with your Precious Blood and fill me with your Holy Spirit.

---

strongest prayer for healing
How to ask God for healing
Psalms 147t 91
Mathew 10:1
3 o'clock prayer

# 3 o'clock Prayer

Implore My mercy, especially for sinners; and, if only for a brief moment, immerse yourself in my Passion, particularly in My abandonment at the moment of agony. This is the hour of great mercy for the whole world.

2) Eternal God, in whom mercy is endless and the treasury of compassion inexhaustible, look kindly upon us and increase your mercy in us, that in difficult moments we might not despair nor become despondent, but with great confidence submit ourselves to your holy will, which is love & mercy itself. Amen

Mathew 10-1

And when he had called unto him his twelve disciples, he gave them power against unclean spirits, to cast them out, and to heal all manner of sickness and all manner of disease.

Printed in the USA
CPSIA information can be obtained
at www.ICGtesting.com
CBHW020743251024
16384CB00021B/40